le soleil

et

la lune

Liv Gibbs

Michael Terence
Publishing

First published in paperback by
Michael Terence Publishing in 2020
www.mtp.agency

Copyright © 2020 Liv Gibbs

Liv Gibbs has asserted the right to be identified as
the author of this work in accordance with the
Copyright, Designs and Patents Act 1988

ISBN 9781913653354

No part of this publication may be reproduced, stored
in a retrieval system, or transmitted, in any form or
by any means, electronic, mechanical, photocopying, recording or
otherwise, without the prior
permission of the publisher

Cover image
Copyright © Mika Besfamilnaya
www.123rf.com

Cover design
Copyright © 2020 Michael Terence Publishing

*for my boy that gave me love and
the people who gave me life*

Contents

1: *Melancolie*.. 1

2: *Brûler*.. 17

3: *Amour* 35

4: *Casser* 67

5: *Épanoui*... 111

6: *Lumière* 121

1:
Melancolie
[a feeling of pensive sadness, typically with no obvious cause]

i am so raw;
the wind
could make me bleed.

i stumble around;
drunk -
yet completely sober.

my biggest fear
is my only saviour.

- *mort*

my heart is so
heavy;
it shackles my feet to the earth.
i watch my mouth move and words
come out. but the voice i hear
is foreign to me.

i am the flower
fallen from the overhanging trees
to the stream
close to home.

drifting,
drifting,

quietly;

slowly.

you were the wind;
the storm
that thrashes and screams and
bites and howls.

my once quiet drift from home:

lay in my grave;
i weep.

my body
and my mind are two.

with my heart at my feet; beating
does it still.

my mind, screaming as my body
falls limp.

quiet.

as my mind falls silent.

my d r u m m i n g heart

may it rest
at last.

to be
a hostage
in your own
rotting
mind.

to feel
so much pain
it becomes numb.

to feel
<u>everything</u>.

to be
hollow

to be

empty

i want the empty to go away.

2:
Brûler
[to burn]

my skies don't rain;
they thunder.

with a
throat of
red raw
wounds

open;

my screams were salt.

i swallow my words;

fire

in my throat.

pour salt in my open wounded
chest, as i drown in the fire
in my veins.

choking on my own blood
with tears of acid burning my cheeks;
scream that **i am not enough**
with *your voice of silk*.

i

am

so

scared.

[help me]

everything i see
is beginning to change, like a
torturously slow deprivation of sight.

what will i do
when i lose what sight
i have left?

once again
the coldness
seeps its way
back into my chest.

my organs
harden into rock.

i welcome
the ice
with quivering arms;
for it is one of the few things
i can always rely
on coming back to me
sooner or later.

- désappointement

i subconsciously seek
a recreation of my past traumas
as a form of self-harming.

3:

Amour

[love]

kisses
so tender
my heart breaks

he sees art within me
where i thought there was none.

"a blank canvas," i say

"a masterpiece," he corrects.

my muscles mimic
the action if embracing you
like an intangible ghost

rose dusted cheeks;
mouth curved;
eyes of stars.

[her]

souls
sewn together gently.

two hearts,
as one.

eyes flickered with galaxies,
crimson painted on his cheeks.

hope
dripping from his words.

you stared at me
as if you were seeing me for the last time;
memorize
every colour and curve.

my eyes
were on the galaxy above.

the moon and i spoke.

i am
forever hers,

despite your lingering eyes.

you asked
if i write about you
i said no.

for the affection i feel for you
is the best damn poetry
i could ever write.

no mere patterns of letters
could do justice
for the extraordinary existence
that is us.

your scent
is my own,
personal drug.

you are my new,
favourite addiction.

and oh,
my god...

how dizzy i feel
after you.

i get high
off the thought of you.

"but honey,
i adore you."

you don't even have to touch
body to make me want you

you could do nothing
and my cells would elite

[the effect of him]

"i mean nothing to anyone"
"you mean everything to me."

to be
utterly besotted
[my infatuation with him]

you asked
if i loved you.

my tongue danced
with a lightness
unknown.

my heart; open.
pouring out liquid gold.

'loving you' i mused,

'is what i was born to do.'

4:
Casser
[to break]

19:51 P.M.
i want you here
even with
the streams of salt
steadily pouring down my
crimson cheeks.

i want you here
in spite of my inability
to tear my eyes
away from my window;

i am yearning to see
your silhouette -
to see you
once again.

23:56 P.M.
why aren't you here?

i am

filled with organs,

yet why
do i feel
so

hollow?

The nights
are always the worst.
the silence howls
in grief.

you were in love
with the idea of me.

the portrayal of a girl;
i externalize
to hide
the fragile creature
within my bones.

you were in love
with the idea of loving me.

but,
when the lies were stripped,
my-self:
naked;
real;
raw.

you ran.

i hate you
because my throat is still raw
from the endless nights
i spent screaming over the loss of you.

i hate you
for even with the arms
around me,
it is
your heart
i hear beating
in my bones.

i hate you
in spite of the
lingering sensation
your kisses left.

i hate you
as the ghost of your touch
shadows over every curve, cut and crevice
of my very being.

i hate you

because i don't.

i hate

that i love you.

i mourn
the part of my heart
that was yours

oh,
how that has
shrivelled
and died.

burnt alive:
with the acid
upon your
heinous tongue -

i watch 'us'
burn to ashes.

my heart bleeds
for the boy you used to be.
i don't know you.
did i ever?

did i fall in love
with a facade?
a faked, outwards exterior;
an external projection
of whom
i wanted you to be -
who you
wanted to be?

or

did you lose something?
a part of you,
when you lost me too.

my love for you has drained away -
so
so
slowly.

but inevitably
and irrevocably,
my love has decayed
and died
when we did too.

hurt me more.

for you
can no longer get
anything else from me.

make me scream in anger,
as i will never praise your name again.

make me bite my lip from sorrow;
the lips you once kissed.

watch my tears
fall down
the cheeks you used to hold.

embarrass me.
ruin me.
kill the part of me –
the idiotic,
immortal flame
that still burns for you:

for us.

what is it like
being with her?

are her kisses
as soft as mine?
do they taste of sugar
and all things devine.

does her voice
shake with vulnerability
when she says she loves you?
or is it only
when she moans your name
that you can evoke such emotions.

is her skin
like silk against your fingertips
the way my body
would mould into yours
like a puzzle you didn't know
when incomplete until now

how does it feel
to lose
the best goddamn thing
that'll ever happen to you?

i hope it hurts like hell
because god knows
you've shown me
what that feels like.

bitter-sweet blood
runs through my veins
when i think of you.

you reside
in the moments of silence
i find when i am left alone with myself.

my mind's favourite game
is a bitter-sweet trick
called *nostalgia*.

everything is in the air
tonight.
i cling onto
the fragile string of hope
for it is all
that is keeping me above water.

my heart,
is in my throat,
my organs
in a panicked frenzy.

fingers, twitching uncontrollably
for all i can do now
is wait.
i've poured my heart and tears
and aching body to you

i'm sorry baby,
for i can be careless with my tongue.
my mouth can be
both sugar and poison.
the words that poured from my lips
were acid elite.

i always
mess it up.

the tension
fogged the air
that we breathed
and left our lungs
heaving for breath.

either break
my heart
or kiss me

i feel
too deeply
to accept the uncertainty.

his hands; selfish things
touching everywhere of him
where i cannot
i envy
his palms,
fingertips,
his bones, bruises and brain

for they all get to be
where i cannot

i always know
it is my mother
walking past my door
late at night.
the banging of the ice,
like a sickly-sweet lullaby,
against the wall
of her glass of liquor.

followed by a heaved sigh;
a sigh filled with so much sadness
my stomach churns,
exhaling the desperation
and how simply
<u>exhausted</u>
she is.

the hurting:
it is in my blood.

craving
tastes like copper
residing in the base of my tongue

the bitter taste of
addiction
weighs like a small stone
in my throat's centre.

a head of hollows.
spoon feed the children of the starved
with the intracranial contents
within my rotting head

the voices scream in the silence

and

i gather all the courage i have left
with trembling bones.
and breathe a sigh of relief
a sigh so hard my ribs crack.
i sign out
my last bit of love for you.

5:
Épanoui
[blooming]

life
bloomed from her death

[to mourn myself]

my body
combusts
and shatters

into *galaxies*.

i am a
murderer;
mourning my own victim.

[to let them go]

i have always felt
so much love
pouring out of me in buckets.

my love has been misplaced,
misused,
abused,
and taken for granted.

i have
so much love to give
yet no one to give it to.

i thought
you were the answer.
i drowned you in affection
and in return
you left me dry.

but

as the drought has passed,
and the deplorable flood has
settled,
i have now learned
where all that love
was finally meant to go:

<u>me</u>.

6:
Lumière
[light]

you challenge me
as you know no different.
my inability
to comply
makes you uncomfortable.

i scare you
with my blunt mouth
and my need
to disregard
your desires.

i will not
be silenced.

i am not a doll -
an object of external envy
with a sole purpose of amplifying
your male dominance.

i will not be complacent
with your
heinous words.

the fire
in my veins,
and the power
in my voice
scares you so.

i will not
dress;
behave;
interact;
or simply be
anything that i am not
just because my self-awareness
frightens you

my strength scares you.
and so it should.

- féminisme

be careful
hanging out your sorries
they carry more depth than you know.

to love myself,

in a systematic hierarchy of self-depreciation that society has enforced to normalize,

is the most radical form
of empowerment

rebel.
rise.
be the anarchy
of the revolution

of loving yourself.

the day
i stop fighting
is the day you take my voice away:

but even with
no vocal cords
or found in a sudden illiterate state

the fire that burns in my belly –
the irrevocable need for change

can never be extinguished i will
never stop fighting.

my heart
pours out kindness
like honey

words;
melt from my lips
that could make you cry
with admiration
for yourself

to be
kind
is the rarest gift
one can possess.

it does not come
from a life -
an upbringing of purity and happiness.
i am learning
to love myself, birthed
from years
of bitterness and self-hatred.

i know
i will hurt
when we inevitably move on.

i know
my heart will ache
for a time i cannot predict.

for the breaking
will tear me -
but it will not kill me.

i have learned to live for me;
with enough love for myself
to fuel a lifetime.

the love i shared with you -
i did not take it from the love from me
but made more.

the same way
a mother's love does not divide
when having children,
but simply grow in size.

A Message from Liv Gibbs

At the age of 12, I began writing some of the poems included in this book. I continued to channel my internalized torture into poetry, oblivious that my bleeding soul would eventually be read by others.

The sad truth to my story is that it is simply one of many. Childhood traumas skinned the innocence from me until I was left a fragile pile of bones. My willingness to persevere came from those around me, to whom let me down incessantly. My heart bled dejection; I craved companionship like starvation.

My frail, credulous heart never hardened, and for that I am thankful. It is my tenderness that allows me to feel everything. Thank you to all who have hurt me. It is you who has given me the strength to live, for me.

My only hope after reading my work is that you find the courage within.

It will be okay.

You will heal.

Find the courage to take a deep breath and sign out your pain.

It is needed no longer.

You have carried the hurting for far too long.

*Available worldwide from all good
high street and online bookstores*

----

www.mtp.agency

www.facebook.com/mtp.agency

@mtp_agency

www.ingramcontent.com/pod-product-compliance
Lightning Source LLC
LaVergne TN
LVHW011713060526
838200LV00051B/2894